PREPARING FOR CHRISTMAS
With Richard Rohr

PREPARING FOR CHRISTMAS
With *Richard Rohr*

Daily Meditations for Advent

ST. ANTHONY MESSENGER PRESS
Cincinnati, Ohio

Great Themes of Paul: Life as Participation

Healing Our Violence Through the Journey of Centering Prayer (with Thomas Keating, O.C.S.O.)

Letting Go: A Spirituality of Subtraction

Men and Women: The Journey of Spiritual Transformation

New Great Themes of Scripture

Preparing for Christmas With Richard Rohr

Rebuild the Church

Richard Rohr on Church: Collected Talks: Volume Three

Richard Rohr on Scripture: Collected Talks: Volume Two

Richard Rohr on Transformation: Collected Talks: Volume One

Sermon on the Mount

A Spirituality for the Two Halves of Life (with Paula D'Arcy)

True Self, False Self

RESCRIPT

In accord with the *Code of Canon Law,* I hereby grant my permission to publish *Preparing for Christmas With Richard Rohr* by Richard Rohr, O.F.M.

Reverend Joseph R. Binzer
Vicar General
Archdiocese of Cincinnati
Cincinnati, Ohio
June 5, 2008

The permission to publish is a declaration that a book of pamphlet is considered to be free from doctrinal or moral error. It is not implied that those who have granted the permission to publish agree with the contents, opinions or statements expressed.

Scripture texts cited at the top of each daily mediation in this work have been taken from *New Revised Standard Version Bible,* copyright ©1989 by the Division of Christian Education of the National Council of the churches of Christ in the U.S.A., and used by permission. All rights reserved. Scripture within the meditations themselves are the author's own translation or paraphrase.

Cover design: Mark Sullivan
Cover photo/image: www.istockphoto.com/Jaap Hart
Interior design: Jennifer Tibbits

Library of Congress Cataloging-in-Publication Data

Rohr, Richard.
  Preparing for Christmas with Richard Rohr : daily reflections for Advent.
      p. cm.
  ISBN 978-0-86716-883-9 (pbk. : alk. paper) 1. Advent—Meditations. 2. Common lectionary (1992) I. Title.
  BV40.R65 2008
  242'.33—dc22

                                    2008024986

ISBN: 978-0-86716-883-9

Published by St. Anthony Messenger Press
28 W. Liberty St.
Cincinnati, OH 45202
www.SAMPBooks.org

Printed in the United States of America.
Printed on acid-free paper.

09 10 11 12 6 5 4 3

Introduction

Some years ago I gave a conference on "Preparing for Christmas" that St. Anthony Messenger Press was kind enough to publish in recorded form. It has continued to sell well for many years, and so they asked me if I would work with them to publish a print version. This booklet is the result.

In the original lectures I tried to invite people beyond a merely sentimental understanding of Christmas as "waiting for the baby Jesus" to an adult and social appreciation of the message of the Incarnation of God in Christ. We Franciscans have always believed that *the Incarnation was already the Redemption*, because in Jesus' birth God was already saying that *it was good to be human, and God was on our side*.

At the original conference, I felt that the need on this earth for adult Christianity and the actual message of Jesus was so urgent that we could not allow this great feast of Christmas, and its preparation in Advent, to be watered down in any way. Twenty years later, I feel this is even more true. Jesus identified his own message with what he called the coming of the "reign of God" or the "kingdom of God," whereas we had often settled for the sweet coming of a baby who asked little of us in terms of surrender, encounter, mutuality or any studying of the Scriptures or the actual teaching of Jesus. Sentimentality, defined as trumped-up emotions, can be an avoiding of and substitute for an actual relationship, as we see in our human relationships, too.

We Catholics must admit that there is a constant temptation among us to avoid the lectionary and the Word of God for private and pious devotions that usually have little power to actually change us or call our ego assumptions into question. The Word of God, however, *confronts, converts and consoles* us—in that order. The suffering, injustice and devastation on this planet are too great now to settle for any infantile gospel or any infantile Jesus. Actually, that has always been true.

"Jesus is Lord!" of all creation! This was the rallying cry of the early church (Philippians 2:11, Acts 2:36, Romans 1:4, etc.). It is to this adult and cosmic Christ that we are saying, "Come, Lord Jesus" (Revelation 22:20), which are the final words of the Bible. This makes our entire lives, and the life of the church, one huge "advent." My hope and prayer is that this little booklet can also do the same. Remember, *Advent is always*–until the end of days.

Peace and every good,
Fr. Richard Rohr, O.F.M.

First Sunday of Advent

Year A: Isaiah 2:1–5; Romans 13:11–14; Matthew 24:37–44

Year B: Isaiah 63:16b–17, 19b; 64:2–7; 1 Corinthians 1:3–9; Mark 13:33–37

Year C: Jeremiah 33:14–16; 1 Thessalonians 3:12—4:2; Luke 21:25–28, 34–36

———

> Keep awake therefore, for you do not
> know on what day your Lord is coming.
>
> —MATTHEW 24:42

COME, LORD JESUS

"Come, Lord Jesus," the Advent mantra, means that all of Christian history has to live out of a kind of deliberate emptiness, a kind of chosen non-fulfillment. Perfect fullness is always to come, and we do not need to demand it now. This keeps the field of life wide open and especially open to grace and to a future created by God rather than ourselves. This is exactly what it means to be "awake," as the Gospel urges us! We can also use other *a* words for

Advent: aware, alive, attentive, alert, awake are all appropriate! Advent is, above all else, a call to full consciousness and a forewarning about the high price of consciousness.

When we demand satisfaction of one another, when we demand any completion to history on our terms, when we demand that our anxiety or any dissatisfaction be taken away, saying as it were, "Why weren't you this for me? Why didn't life do that for me?" we are refusing to say, "Come, Lord Jesus." We are refusing to hold out for the *full picture* that is always given by God.

"Come, Lord Jesus" is a leap into the kind of freedom and surrender that is rightly called the virtue of hope. The theological virtue of hope is the patient and trustful willingness to live without closure, without resolution, and still be content and even happy because our Satisfaction is now at another level, and our Source is beyond ourselves. We are able to trust that he *will* come again, just as Jesus has come into our past, into our private dilemmas and into our suffering world. Our Christian past then becomes our Christian prologue, and "Come, Lord Jesus" is not a cry of desperation but an assured shout of cosmic hope.

REFLECT

What expectations and demands of life can you let go of so that you can be more prepared for the coming of Jesus?

Monday of the First Week of Advent

Isaiah 2:1–5 (Isaiah 4:2–6 for Year A); Matthew 8:5–11

——⁓∭⁓——

> Lord, I am not worthy to have you come
> under my roof; but only speak the word,
> and my servant will be healed.
>
> —MATTHEW 8:8

MAKING ROOM INSIDE

The American Declaration of Independence says we have an "unalienable right" to the pursuit of happiness. God created us to be happy and joyful "in this world and the next," and Jesus says the same several times in John 14–17. The only difference between the two is that any happiness that is *demanded* from life never becomes happiness because it is too narcissistically and self-consciously pursued. The "joy that the world cannot give" (John 14:27) always comes as a gift to those who wait for it, expect it and make room for it inside themselves. The first is self-assertion, the second is self-surrender. The first is taking; the second is receiving. Those are two entirely different human dynamics. You do not catch a butterfly by chasing it: You sit still and it alights on your shoulder. Then it chooses you. That is true happiness.

When we set out to seek our private happiness, we often create an idol that is sure to topple. Any attempts to protect any full and private happiness in the midst of so much public suffering have to be based on illusion about the nature of the world we live in. We can only do that if we block ourselves from a certain degree of reality and refuse solidarity with "the other side" of everything, even the other side of ourselves.

Both sides of life are good and necessary teachers; in fact, failure and mistake teach us much more than our successes. Failure and success were often called "the two hands of God" or the "paschal mystery." It takes struggles with both our darkness and our light to form us into full children of God, but of course, we especially resist "the left hand of God" which is usually some form of suffering (read *loss of control*). As in our Gospel today, it was the same suffering of the centurion's servant that brought the centurion out of his comfortable house and that invited Jesus into that house! Suffering and solidarity with the suffering of others has an immense capacity to "make room" inside of us. It is probably our primary spiritual teacher.

What attachments in your life can you let go of to make more room for God?

Tuesday of the First Week of Advent

Isaiah 11:1–10; Luke 10:21–24

> No one knows who the Son is except the Father, or who the Father is except the Son and anyone to whom the Son chooses to reveal him.
>
> —LUKE 10:22

THE COSMIC CHRIST

The Second Coming of Christ that history is waiting for is not the same as the baby Jesus or even the historical Jesus. The historical Jesus was one man, and Christ is not his last name. *The Christ* includes the whole sweep of creation and history joined with him—and you too. We call this the Cosmic Christ. We ourselves are a member of the Body of

Christ and the Cosmic Christ, even though we are not the historical Jesus. So we very rightly believe in "*Jesus Christ,*" and both words are essential.

The celebration of Christmas is not a sentimental waiting for a baby to be born, but much more *an asking for history to be born!* (See Romans 8:20-23.) We do the Gospel no favor when we make Jesus, the Eternal Christ, into a perpetual baby, a baby able to ask little or no adult response from us. One even wonders what the mind is that would keep Jesus a baby. Maybe it was "baby Christianity."

We might cuddle or coo with a baby, but any spirituality that makes too much of the baby Jesus is perhaps not yet ready for prime-time life. God clearly wants friends, partners and images, if we are to believe the biblical texts. God, it seems, wants adult religion and a mature, free response from us. God loves us as adult partners, with mutual give and take, and *you eventually become the God that you love.* Take that as an absolute.

I understand where such devotions to the Infant of this or that, the *Santo Niño* of here or there, came from; but these do not come close to the power of the biblical proclamation that clearly invites us into adult "cooperation" (Romans 8:28), free "participation" (Philippians 3:10) and the love of free and mature persons in God (Ephesians 4:13). You can apparently trust yourself that much because God has done it first and foremost. The Christ we are asking for and waiting for includes your own full birth and the further birth of history and creation. Now you can say "Come, Christ Jesus" with a whole new understanding and a deliberate passion!

REFLECT

What perceptions of Jesus and Christ do you have that need to be changed?

Wednesday of the First Week of Advent

Isaiah 25:6–10a; Matthew 15:29–37

—⟋⟋⟍—

> On this mountain the LORD of hosts will
> make for all peoples
> a feast of rich food, a feast of well-
> aged wines.
>
> —ISAIAH 25:6

THE KINGDOM ON EARTH

I sometimes feel we preachers and teachers must come up with new sermons all the time. It seems terribly unfair because Jesus basically had one sermon that he just kept saying in different ways. Jesus announced the presence of what he called "the kingdom" or the "reign" of God. He kept saying "it is like" or "it may be compared to" (see Matthew 13), and he used stories, parables and metaphors so that we could recognize what was obvious to him but not so obvious to us. Religion can only use the language of metaphor because we are pointing to transcendent things. Jesus told us to pray that this mystery would be as obvious to us "on earth as it is in heaven." The banquet described in today's Isaiah reading, for example, is clearly *now* and also later. Jesus was asking us to see, to see fully, and to see that the inside of things is always bigger than the mere outside.

Basically, you can translate "the kingdom" as "the Big Picture," which is how I will use it in this booklet. The kingdom of God, or reign of God, is *how things objectively, truly and finally are.* Jesus is always inviting us to live in the final and full picture, and not to get lost in momentary dramas, hurts or agendas. In Latin we used to say *sub specie aeternitate*, that is, to ask ourselves everyday, "In the light of eternity will this really matter?"

There is one Great Drama that utterly relativizes and situates all our daily emotions, hurts, addictions and plans. When you abide in the Godself, the small self is always seen as limited, insecure and good—but still passing away. We must eat from another table to know who we really and finally are. When we can live inside this great inner feast of life, as described so beautifully today by Isaiah, most passing things become exactly that—passing things inside of the Great Banquet of inner aliveness in God.

REFLECT

What study, if any, have you done of the True Self and the false self? You might wish to listen to my audio presentation *True Self, False Self,* available from St. Anthony Messenger Press.

Thursday of the First Week of Advent

Isaiah 26:1–6; Matthew 7:21, 24–27

—⁓〰⁓—

> Not everyone who says to me, "Lord, Lord," will enter the kingdom of heaven, but only the one who does the will of my Father in heaven.
>
> —MATTHEW 7:21

If we try to make the church into the kingdom of God, we create idolatry. I suspect that is what Jesus means by the "Lord, Lord" line. If we try to make this world itself into the kingdom, we will always be resentful and disappointed. If we make heaven into the kingdom, we miss most of its transformative message. We are not waiting for the coming of an ideal church or any perfect world here and now, or even just for the next world. The kingdom is more than all of these. It is always here and not here. It is always now and not yet. No institution can encompass it. That is rather clear in the texts where Jesus describes the kingdom. All false religion proceeds in a certain sense from one illusion. When people say piously, "Thy kingdom come" out of one side of their mouth, they need also to say, "My kingdom go!" out of the other side. The kingdom of God supersedes and far surpasses all kingdoms of self and society or personal reward.

As Jesus says in another place, "No one can serve two masters, he will always love one and ignore the other" (Matthew 6:24). Our first and final loyalty is to one kingdom: God's or our own. We really can't fake it. The Big Picture is apparent when God's work and will is central, and we are happy to take our place in the corner of the frame. This is "doing the will of my Father in heaven" and allows the larger theater of life and love to unfold.

I believe Jesus was teaching a larger version of what many of us say today when we say that we must "think globally and act locally." Because I am a part of the Big Picture, I *do* matter and substantially so. Because I am *only* a part, however, I am rightly situated off to stage right—and happily so. What freedom there is in such truth! *We are inherently important and included, yet not burdened with manufacturing or sustaining that private importance.* Our dignity is given by God, and we are freed from ourselves!

Yet it gets bigger and better because the proclamation of the kingdom of God frees us from social idolatries too. We can't keep saying "Thy kingdom come" when we are actually trusting in our own nations, political parties, militaries, banks and institutions to save us. On some level, they have to be relativized too if the Big Kingdom is ever going to come, which is why Pope John Paul II so often spoke of "structural sin" and "institutional evil." We might "use" the systems of this world, I hope wisely, but we never "believe" in them. We only *believe in* God! Any universal church, any truly "catholic" people should be first in line to understand this: "Come, Lord Jesus" means we do not spend too much time trusting that other "Lordships" will ever finally save us.

What "kingdoms" do you need to let go of before you can enjoy the kingdom of heaven?

Friday of the First Week of Advent

Isaiah 29:17–24; Matthew 9:27–31

—⚬—

> And those who err in spirit will come to
> understanding,
> and those who grumble will accept
> instruction.
>
> —ISAIAH 29:24

ALLOWING GOD'S TRUTH

Jesus clearly says the kingdom of heaven is among us (Luke 17:21) or "at hand" (Matthew 3:2, 4:17). One wonders why we made it into a reward system for later, or as someone called it, "a divine evacuation plan" from this world. Maybe it was easier to obey laws and practice rituals for later reward than to actually be transformed now.

The price for real transformation is high. It means that we have to change our loyalties from power, success, money and control (read: "our kingdoms") to the Lordship of Jesus and the kingdom of God. Henceforth, there is only one thing that is Absolute and, in relationship to that, everything else is relative—*everything*—even the church (Don't think I am disloyal because the failure to understand this is what got many of our leaders into trouble recently), even our nation, even national security, even our wealth and our possessions, even our identity and our reputation. All of our safety nets must now be of secondary or even tertiary importance, or even let go of, because Jesus is Lord! Whatever you trust to validate you and secure you is your real god, and the Gospel is saying, "Will the real God please stand up?"

We can see why there are so few kingdom people. Jesus is saying that all these systems are passing away and limited and that we should not put all of our eggs into such baskets. Yes, we need to work inside of these institutions for social order and some small degree of justice, but we shouldn't think these systems will ever of themselves accomplish God's justice or God's reign. If a person thinks this, he or she will end up bitter by the second half of life.

What in your life gives you false happiness and fulfillment and prevents you from letting God's truth break into your life?

Saturday of the First Week of Advent

Isaiah 30:19–21, 23–26; Matthew 9:35—10:1, 5a, 6–8

> Go rather to the lost sheep of the house of
> Israel. As you go, proclaim the good news,
> "The kingdom of heaven has come near."
>
> —MATTHEW 10:6-7

JESUS, A RADICAL REFORMER

The recognition of the Big Picture is probably as rare in our age as it was in the time of Jesus. Why should it be any different? Even the twelve apostles had trouble with it. It is never going to be popular. It is never going to be for the masses—unless they are awake and aware. Otherwise, they will usually substitute a perfect society, heaven or the church for the True and Big Picture. We live in the in-between and with an excess of hope because *there is just enough of "now" to assure us of the "not yet."*

Jesus gave the world a counter-intuitive message that is necessary for depth and ongoing reform in all of the world's religions. He was a radical reformer of his own Jewish religion, and in that, all religions, *which normally follow Judaism's classic patterns of both getting the message and utterly opposing their own message.* Unfortunately, we applied all of Jesus' criticisms (see Matthew 23) to "those incorrigible and hard hearted Jews" and forgot that the same criticisms apply to Catholicism, Orthodoxy and every Protestant reform of the last five hundred years. We are each and all *now and not yet, and we all live in the in-between.*

In today's Gospel, Jesus appears to be reaching out to the "lost sheep of the house of Israel" and trying to bring them back to authentic Judaism (not at that point, to a new religion!), but that authenticity itself became Christianity or "the good news" for many who were awake and aware. Yet now we can join "the new Israel" and still be lost sheep all over again because the patterns of delusion are the same in every age and every religion.

REFLECT

What misperceptions do you have about God's kingdom? What perspectives do you need to gain?

Second Sunday of Advent

Year A: Isaiah 11:1–10; Romans 15:4–9; Matthew 3:1–12

Year B: Isaiah 40:1–5, 9–11; 2 Peter 3:8–14; Mark 1:1–8

Year C: Baruch 5:1–9; Philippians 1:4–6, 8–11; Luke 3:1–6

He proclaimed, "The one who is more
powerful than I is coming after me; I am
not worthy to stoop down and untie the
thong of his sandals. I have baptized you
with water; but he will baptize you with
the Holy Spirit."

—MARK 1:7–8

JOHN, THE MASTER OF DESCENT

John the Baptist's qualities are most rare and yet crucial for
any reform or authentic transformation of persons or groups.
That is why we focus on John the Baptist every Advent and
why Jesus trusts him and accepts his non-temple, offbeat
nature ritual, while also going far beyond him. Water is only

the container; fire and Spirit are the contents, John says. Yet if we are not like the great John, we will invariably substitute our own little container for the real contents. We will substitute rituals for reality instead of letting the rituals point us beyond themselves.

John the Baptizer is the strangest combination of conviction and humility, morality and mysticism, radical prophecy and living in the present. This son of the priestly temple class does his own thing down by the riverside; he is a man born into privilege who dresses like a hippie; he is a superstar who is willing to let go of everything, creating his own water baptism and then saying that what really matters is the baptism of "Spirit and fire"! He is a living paradox, as even Jesus says of him: "There is no man greater than John...but he is also the least" in the new reality that I am bringing about (Matthew 11:11). John both gets it and does not get it at all, which is why he has to exit stage right early in the drama. He has played his single and important part, and he knows it. His is brilliantly a spirituality of descent, not ascent. "He must grow bigger, I must grow smaller" (John 3:30).

The only way such freedom can happen is if John learned to be very empty of himself already as a young man, before he even built his tower of success. His ego was out of the way so much so that he could let go of his own ego, his own message and even his own life. This is surely the real meaning of his head on a platter! Some have cleverly said that ego is an acronym for "Edging God Out." There's got to be such emptiness, or we cannot point beyond ourselves to Jesus, as John did. Such emptiness doesn't just fall into our laps; such humility does not just happen. It is surely the end product of a thousand letting-goes and a thousand acts of devotion, which for John the Baptist gradually edged God *in*.

REFLECT

How is your spirituality one of ascent or descent?

Monday of the Second Week of Advent

Isaiah 35:1–10; Luke 5:17–26

—ww—

> Steadfast love and faithfulness will meet;
> righteousness and peace will kiss
> each other.

> Faithfulness will spring up from the ground,
> and righteousness will look down
> from the sky.
>
> —PSALM 85:10–11

WAITING IN DARKNESS

The darkness will never totally go away. I've worked long enough in ministry to know that darkness isn't going to disappear, but that, as John's Gospel says, "the light shines on inside of the darkness, and the darkness will not overcome it" (1:5). Such is the Christian form of yin-yang, our own belief in paradox and mystery.

We must all hope and work to eliminate darkness, especially in many of the great social issues of our time. We wish world hunger could be eliminated. We wish we could stop wasting the earth's resources on armaments. We wish we could stop killing people from womb to tomb. But at a certain point, we have to surrender to the fact that the darkness has always been here, and the only real question is how to receive the light and spread the light. That is not capitulation any more than the cross was capitulation. It is real transformation into the absolutely unique character and program of the Risen Christ.

What we need to do is recognize what is, in fact, darkness and then learn how to live in creative and courageous relationship to it. In other words, don't name darkness *light*. Don't name darkness *good,* which is the seduction that has happened to many of our people on both left and right. They have not been taught wisdom or discernment for the most part. The most common way to release our inner tension is to cease calling darkness *darkness* and to pretend it is passable light. Another way to release your inner tension is to stand angrily, obsessively against it, but then you become a mirror image of it. Everyone can usually see this but you!

Our Christian wisdom is to name the darkness as darkness, and the Light as light, and to learn how to live and work in the Light so that the darkness does not overcome us. If we have a pie-in-the-sky, everything-is-beautiful attitude, we are in fact going to be trapped by the darkness because we are not seeing clearly enough to separate the wheat from the chaff (the more common "liberal" temptation). Conversely, if we can only see the darkness and forget the more foundational Light, we will be destroyed by our own negativity and fanaticism, or we will naively think we are *apart from the darkness* (the more common "conservative" temptations). Instead, we must wait and work with hope inside of the darkness—while never doubting the light that God always is—and that we are too (Matthew 5:14). That is the narrow birth canal of God into the world—*through* the darkness and into an ever greater Light.

REFLECT

In what parts of your life are you trying to push away darkness instead of living with it as a teacher and transformer?

Tuesday of the Second Week of Advent

Isaiah 40:1–11; Matthew 18:12–14

—⟋⟋⟍—

> It is not the will of your Father in heaven
> that one of these little ones should be lost.
> —MATTHEW 18:14

BACK TO FAITH

I served as a jail chaplain in Albuquerque for fourteen years. It was so rewarding to preach to the guys and gals in the jail. They don't have all of this heady sophistication that I have learned. They're not lost in worlds of words, whereby everything is made vague. It is very clear to them what death is; it is very clear to them *what* is destroying people and sometimes *how* it is destroying people. There simply is not the same kind of self-protection or capacity for denial in their souls because they have all been to the bottom. I could always talk real in the jail, whereas in parishes I often had to talk "nice."

Each Sunday morning at the jail I celebrated three Masses, and the third one was with the women. Jailed women always feel so bad about themselves. Society holds the common notion that men are supposed to go to jail; men are bad. But society says women aren't bad; women are good; women have children; women are empathetic; women don't go to jail. Yet women in jail carry a lot of guilt and shame. They often asked me, "Why am I here? What is wrong with me?" The women felt so guilty because their children were at home, and these mothers were in jail. How could a mother tell her children that she is in jail and let her children think that Mom is a bad person?

These women must dig into places inside themselves that you and I don't have to dig into. Religion of itself is not enough for such women and men. These women and men must scratch their way back to faith, and when they get there, it is often the real thing. We always said,

"Religion is for people who are afraid of hell or afraid of God, whereas spirituality is for people who have been through hell and 'undergone' God."

We nice guys don't usually have to scratch our way back to faith. We're comfortable with external religion and polite morality for a long time. God will lead each of us, I am sure, but by a different path, so that all religion one day has to be faith, love, humility and surrender—or it is not true religion! None of God's "little ones will be lost." And we are "one of these little ones" too, just in a different way.

REFLECT

When have you been so lost that you've had to go back to the very foundations of your faith?

Wednesday of the Second Week of Advent

Isaiah 40:25–31; Matthew 11:28–30

—〰—

> Come to me, all you that are weary and
> are carrying heavy burdens, and I will give
> you rest.
>
> —MATTHEW 11:28

It is safe to say that there is confusion about what is *needed* for life and what is really *important* for life. The vast majority of American stores seem to be selling *wants* not *needs*. What we now call needs were formerly wants, and they have moved to such a level of sophistication that now luxuries are "necessities" for many of us. The upwardly mobile in our culture cannot feel good about themselves unless the vacation next year is more luxurious than last year's, unless the clothes and the house are upgraded, unless the latest gadget is acquired. This keeps us all quite trapped and un-free, and inherently unsatisfied. We are running on a perpetual hamster's wheel.

Meanwhile, most of God's people on this earth starve; most of God's people have to learn to find happiness and learn to find freedom at a much simpler level. What the Gospel is saying, of course, is that such simplicity is the only place that happiness is ever to be found in the first place. We have moved to a level where we have made happiness and contentment largely impossible. We have created a pseudo-happiness, largely based in *having* instead of *being*. We are so overstimulated that the ordinary no longer delights us. We cannot rest or abide in our *naked being in God*, as Jesus offers us.

Such a message is about as traditional, old-fashioned and conservative a gospel as we can possibly preach, and it will always be true. Every generation needs to hear it and believe this anew, but particularly in our time and culture when even middle-class people have more comforts and securities than did kings and queens in the times when royalty flourished. We have become human *doings* more than human *beings*, and the verb "rest," as Jesus uses it, is largely foreign to us. Indeed, such rest feels like "nothing" at all, which makes it very hard to sell to people who do not value rest.

REFLECT

What in your life, material or not, are you using to fulfill a need that really should be sought from elsewhere?

Thursday of the Second Week of Advent

Isaiah 41:13–20; Matthew 11:11–15

—⁓—

Let anyone with ears listen!

—MATTHEW 11:15

GREAT LOVE AND GREAT SUFFERING

It is increasingly striking to me how much Jesus talks about seeing, hearing, listening and not being blind, as in today's Gospel. I used to think he was just pointing to hard-hearted and wicked people, certainly not ordinary folks like you and me. The longer I have worked with people, however, the more I see that it is cultural and institutional blindness that keeps most of us from deeper seeing, and not usually personal bad will. We mostly think like everybody around us thinks unless we have taken some real inner journeys of love, prayer and suffering. Without great love and/or great suffering, human consciousness remains largely at the fight-or-flight, either/or, all-or-nothing level. This dualistic mind, that we can now prove is the lowest level of brain function, will never be able to access, much less deal with, the really big things that are invariably "mysterious."

What are the big things? I would list love, freedom, evil, God, eternity, nonviolence, forgiveness, grace and mercy. These the dualistic mind cannot comprehend, and in fact, it usually gets them utterly wrong because they each have a paradoxical character that demands some degree of non-dual thinking.

Jesus is talking today to all of us, and not just to those really bad people out there. We can be very sincere, good-willed and even want to be loving, but the big issues will still bring us to the blindness and deafness that Jesus talks about. It is largely great love and great suffering that create spiritual listening and larger seeing. Mere belief systems and church services do not of themselves assure such transformation. This is surely why Jesus criticizes the people's inability to understand the law and the prophets in today's Gospel, which they all "believed in" but did not really understand at all. Note that Jesus is not talking to the bad guys here but just to "the people" (Matthew 11:7).

REFLECT

Do you tend to think dualistically? Does it help you to be more loving? Does it help you to be more obedient to the gospel?

Friday of the Second Week of Advent

Isaiah 48:17–19; Matthew 11:16–19

—⁓—

> O that you had paid attention to my
>   commandments!
>   Then your prosperity would have been like
>   a river,
>   and your success like the waves of the sea;
> your offspring would have been like the sand,

and your descendants like its grains;
their name would never be cut off
or destroyed from before me.

—ISAIAH 48:18–19

MARY, PERFECT IMAGE OF FRUITFULNESS

How do we also give birth, as Mary did?

We tend to manage life more than just live it. We are all overstimulated and drowning in options. We are trained to be managers, to organize life, to make things happen. That is what built our culture. It is not all bad, but if you transfer that to the spiritual life, it is pure heresy. It is wrong. It doesn't work. It is not gospel. We might be economically rich but not spiritually fertile, as Isaiah teaches. If Mary was trustfully carrying Jesus during this time, it is because she knew how to receive spiritual gifts, in fact *the* spiritual gift. She is probably the perfect image of how fertility and fruitfulness break into this world.

We can't manage, maneuver or manipulate spiritual energy. It is a matter of letting go and receiving what is being given freely. It is the gradual emptying of our attachment to our small self so that there is room for a new conception and a new birth. There must be some displacement before there can be any new "replacement"! Mary is the archetype of such self-displacement and surrender. If Jesus is the symbol of the gift itself and how God gives the gift, then Mary is the symbol of how the gift is received and treasured. Whatever God gives is always experienced as totally unearned grace and never as a salary, a reward or a merit badge of any sort. In fact, if you do experience it that way, it is not from God and will not expand your heart, mind or soul.

There is no mention of any moral worthiness, achievement or preparedness in Mary, only humble trust and surrender. She gives us all, therefore, a bottomless hope in our own little state. If we ourselves try to "manage" God, or manufacture our own worthiness by any performance principle whatsoever, we will never bring forth the Christ but only ourselves. Mary does not manage, fix, control or "perform" in any way. She just says "yes!" and brings forth the abundance that Isaiah promises ("river," "waves," sands of the seashore). This is really quite awesome!

REFLECT

How can you receive instead of manage life? How does managing give you a sense of importance? How does receiving give you a sense of unimportance?

Saturday of the Second Week of Advent

Sirach 48:1–4, 9–11; Matthew 17:9a, 10–13

—⟋⟍—

> Therefore do not worry, saying, "What will
> we eat?" or "What will we drink?" or "What
> will we wear?" For it is the Gentiles who
> strive for all these things; and indeed your
> heavenly Father knows that you need all
> these things. But strive first for the king-
> dom of God and his righteousness, and all
> these things will be given to you as well.
>
> —MATTHEW 6:31-33

LESS IS MORE

I have never been busier in my life than I have been
recently. What right do I have to talk about contemplation
when I have been living on overdrive? It seems that we
tend to think that more is better. I am told that busyness is
actually a status symbol for us! It is strange that when people have so much, they are so anxious about not having
enough—to do, to see, to own, to fix, to control, to change.

Several years ago when I was in Nicaragua, I asked a man if he had time, and he said, "I have the rest of my life," and smiled. Who of us would possibly say that? That is what we don't have. What we don't have is the rest of our lives because we do not even have the *now* of our lives. The decisions we have made in our past have decided our tomorrows; the credit cards and mortgages, the planned obsolescence of almost everything we own, is keeping us all running. And we are not sure why. We don't have the rest of our lives. They are all determined. They are all assured, insured and worried about ahead of time.

We have grown up with all sorts of time-saving devices, and undoubtedly some of us will receive even more of them at Christmas, perhaps finding under our Christmas trees a waffle maker to save time at breakfast or a bun warmer to make dinner preparation faster. Once we own these devices, then we build bigger kitchens that require more cleaning and more energy to store more of our time-saving devices. All these things will save us time—not!

Time is exactly what we do not have. What decreases in a culture of affluence is precisely and strangely *time*—along with wisdom and friendship. These are the very things that the human heart was created for, that the human heart feeds on and lives for. No wonder we are producing so many depressed, unhealthy and even violent people, while also leaving a huge carbon footprint on this poor planet.

Jesus said it to us quite clearly: "Why are you so anxious? Why do you run after things like the pagans do? What shall I eat? What shall I wear? You are not to worry about tomorrow. Each day will take care of itself." (Matthew 6:31, 34). But for some reason, mostly what we do is reprocess the past and worry about tomorrow. This must tell us that we have not understood the spiritual message of Jesus very well. Now the very earth is telling us so.

REFLECT

What one or two things do you need to do well? What do you have to stop doing to do that?

Third Sunday of Advent

Year A: Isaiah 35:1–6a, 10; James 5:7–10; Matthew 11:2–11

Year B: Isaiah 61:1–2a, 10–11; 1 Thessalonians 5:16–24; John
            1:6–8, 19–28

Year C: Zephaniah 3:14–18a; Philippians 4:4–7; Luke 3:10–18

—————

> The spirit of the Lord God is upon me...he
> has sent me to bring good news to the
> oppressed, to bind up the brokenhearted,
> to proclaim liberty to the captives, and
> release to the prisoners.
>
> —ISAIAH 61:1

RELATED IN THE SPIRIT

The Spirit always connects, reconciles, forgives, heals and
makes two into one. It moves beyond human-made boundaries to utterly realign and renew that which is separated
and alienated. The "diabolical" (from two Greek words, *dia*

balein, that mean "to throw apart"), by contrast, always divides and separates that which could be united and at peace. Just as the Spirit always makes one out of two, so the evil one invariably makes two out of one! The evil one tears the fabric of life apart, while the Spirit comes to mend, soften and heal.

In today's reading from Isaiah, the prophet describes the coming Servant of Yahweh. It is precisely this quote that Jesus first uses to announce the exact nature of his own ministry (Luke 4:18-19). In each case Jesus describes his work as moving outside of polite and proper limits and boundaries to reunite things that have been marginalized or excluded by society: the poor, the imprisoned, the blind, the downtrodden. His ministry is not to gather the so-called good into a private country club but to reach out to those on the edge and on the bottom, those who are "last" to tell them they are, in fact, first! That is almost the very job description of the Holy Spirit, and therefore of Jesus.

The more that we can put together, the more that we can "forgive" and allow, the more we can include and enjoy, the more we tend to be living in the Spirit. The more we need to reject, oppose, deny, exclude and eliminate, the more open we are to negative and destructive voices and to our own worst instincts. As always, Jesus is our model of healing, outreach and reconciliation, the ultimate man of the Spirit.

Reflect

What divisions exist in your life? How can you let the Spirit mend those divisions?

Monday of the Third Week of Advent

Numbers 24:2–7, 15–17a; Matthew 21:23–27

——〰——

> So they answered Jesus, "We do not
> know." And he said to them, "Neither will I
> tell you by what authority I am doing
> these things."
>
> —Matthew 21:27

Non-dual Thinking

Can we care intensely and passionately and not care at all in the same moment? If we are seeking God's will and not our own, it comes somewhat easily. We do the best we can, but we are detached from any need for personal success or response. We can then care and not care in the same moment. That is true spiritual freedom.

Can we even understand such a concept anymore? Does it sound like doubletalk? All great spiritual doctrines invariably have the character of paradox to them. For example, we believe that Jesus is human and divine at the same time. Mary is virgin and mother at the same time. The Eucharist is bread and Jesus at the same time. God is both three and one at the same time. These are all logical contradictions, so the rational mind has to go elsewhere to comprehend. Things can be true on one level, and on another not true at all. Wisdom is to know how to hear and see on different levels at the same time, as Jesus so cleverly does in today's Gospel. He is a classic non-dual thinker who knows how to deal creatively with mystery, paradox and negative people too. We cannot love, forgive or be patient if we are totally dualistic.

Jesus refuses to lend himself to hostile, dualistic thinkers who present him with a false dichotomy. As he often does in such cases, Jesus keeps quiet, changes the subject, tells a story, reframes the whole question or just refuses to engage with obvious ill will. He knows that a person becomes a mirror image of anything if he opposes it in kind. So here Jesus just refuses to answer. Amazing that we made

Jesus into the consummate answer giver because that is not what he usually does. He more often leads us right onto the horns of our own human-made dilemmas, where we are forced to meet God and be honest with ourselves. He creates problems for us more than resolves them, problems that very often cannot be resolved by all-or-nothing thinking but only by love and forgiveness.

Reflect

What are the seemingly irresolvable paradoxes in your life? How do you deal with them emotionally? Intellectually? Spiritually?

Tuesday of the Third Week of Advent

Zephaniah 3:1–2, 9–13; Matthew 21:28–32

> Truly I tell you, the tax collectors and the
> prostitutes are going into the kingdom of
> God ahead of you. For John came to you
> in the way of righteousness and you did
> not believe him, but the tax collectors and

the prostitutes believed him; and even
after you saw it, you did not change your
minds and believe him.

—MATTHEW 21:31B-32

THE IMITATION OF GOD

Here is Jesus talking in riddles again. If I spoke or wrote in such a way, you would probably accuse me of moral relativism or fuzzy thinking! How do we learn to live with such confusions?

We must first be willing to admit the contradictions inside us, and still let God love us in that partial state. Once we agree to see our own shadow side, our own foolishness, our own sin and still know that God has not abandoned us, we become a living paradox that reveals the goodness of God. This is what the tax collectors and prostitutes had to do, and what changed them. Notice that the "nice people" were unwilling to "change their minds" about themselves or about God. Once we know that God lives inside our contradictions, and God's love is not dependent on our perfection, then other peoples' contradictions don't scandalize us or surprise us anymore. Henceforward we can be much more patient and compassionate with others because we have allowed God to do the same with us! Basically, the

Christian moral life is no more and no less than "the imitation of God" (Ephesians 5:1).

I am a mass of contradictions and yet I am also a saint. I am a very good person, and I am also a sinful person. I get it and yet I oppose it too. Are both of those true? Yes, both are always and forever true, and for some wonderful reason that is what God loves. Faith is to personally surrender to such a mystery—not on a theoretical level, but right inside ourselves on a daily level. The poor prostitutes had no choice, and if we are honest, we don't either. That is what I mean by "living yourself into a new way of thinking." *Every change of mind is first of all a change of heart, and if the heart does not change, new ideas do not last long.* We all "know the mystery of salvation by the forgiveness of sin," as Saint Luke said (1:77), because forgiveness is not something God does, it is who God is. There is probably no other way to understand God's nature except to daily stand under the waterfall of divine mercy and then become conduits of the same flow.

REFLECT

Can you name at least one of your own inner contradictions? Do you think God can still love you? Can you love yourself?

Wednesday of the Third Week of Advent

Isaiah 45:6c–8, 18, 21c–25; Luke 7:18b–23

—⁂—

Only in the LORD...are righteousness and
strength...
In the LORD all the offspring of Israel shall
triumph and glory.

—ISAIAH 45:24, 25

SELF-IMAGE

One of the major problems in the spiritual life is our attachment to our own self-image—either positively or negatively created. We have to begin with some kind of identity, but the trouble is that we confuse this *idea* of ourselves with who we actually *are* in God. Ideas about things are not the things in themselves. We all have to start by forming a self-image, but the problem is our attachment to it, our need to promote it and protect it and have others like it. What a trap!

Fortunately, that is what the Spirit has to strip away from us so that we can find our "triumph and glory," as Isaiah says, in God's image of us rather than in our image of ourselves, which is always changing anyway. Who we are in God (Galatians 2:20-21) is a much more enduring and solid foundation. I always say that I will take God's kind judgment of me any day over my usually harsh judgment of myself. I will take God's image of me any day, which is always patient and merciful, over my neighbor's rashly formed image of me. *God always sees his son, Jesus, in me, and cannot* not *love him!* (See John 17:22-23.) This is a solid and enduring self-image—no up and down anymore.

When I started in ministry in the early 1970s in Cincinnati and worked with young people, it seemed like I spent most of the time trying to convince teenagers that they were good. They all seemed to endlessly hate themselves. Later I saw it was adults, too, who forever doubted and feared themselves. They had to spend much of their energy, to use the American phrase, trying to "feel good about themselves." Their self-image was based on mere psychological information instead of theological truth. What the Gospel promises us is that we *are objectively and inherently children of God* (see 1 John 3:2). This is not psychological worthiness; it is ontological, metaphysical and substantial, and cannot be gained or lost. When this given God image becomes our self-image, we are home free, and the Gospel is just about the best good news that we can hope for!

I am convinced that so much guilt, low, negative self-image, self-hatred and self-preoccupation occurs because we have allowed our Christian people to be at home in a world, to take their cues and identity from a world, that Jesus told us never to take as normative to begin with! As John says, "Why do you look to one another for approval instead of the approval that comes from the one God?" (5:44). So many of us accept either a successful or a negative self-image *inside of a system of false images to begin with!* This will never work. We must find our true self "hidden with Christ in God" as Paul says (Colossians 3:3). Or as Teresa of Avila put it, *"Find God in yourself, and find yourself in God."* Then we do not go up and down, but we are built on the Rock of Ages.

REFLECT

Which of your self-images (positive or negative) get in the way of your relationship with God? Whenever we get defensive or go emotionally up and down, this is a sign that we are attached to a self-image.

Thursday of the Third Week of Advent

Isaiah 54:1–10; Luke 7:24–30

—ⱳⱳ—

> What did you go out into the wilderness
> to look at? A reed shaken by the wind?
>
> —LUKE 7:24

WHAT YOU SEEK IS WHAT YOU FIND

Where do we look? When will it come?

We all tend to aim for the goal instead of the journey itself, but spiritually speaking, *how we get there is where we arrive.* The journey determines the final destination. If we manipulate our way, we end up with a manipulated, self-made god. If we allow ourselves to be drawn and chosen by love, we might just end up with the real God. But we are all looking for quick methods and techniques to "get God" almost as if God could be an ego possession, a personal trophy. Farther on in this same Gospel, both the Pharisees and the disciples ask Jesus, "When and where will the kingdom come?" (Luke 17:20-22). Jesus says, "The kingdom of God does not admit of observation. Don't believe those who say Lo Here, Lo There."

In other words, it is not going to be easily and obviously localized like those who are looking for an answer man in the desert. Jesus warns people they will be disappointed because *they are looking for the wrong thing by looking for the whole thing right now.* Jesus says, John is both "the greatest" and yet "the least" (7:28). The message is: Yes, this is the kingdom, but it is also not entirely the kingdom. Yes, it is here, but not totally here. It is there, but not entirely there. The kingdom will never be a private ego possession of anyone. None of us is worthy, and in fact, worthiness is not even the issue. Only trust. No one can say, "I have it." It is always an invitation, just enough to draw us deeper. Just enough of God to make us want more of God, but God is always in the driver's seat. "You have not chosen me, I am always choosing you" (John 15:16).

But, thank God, Luke ends that very passage by saying, "The kingdom of God is in your midst" (17:21). The Gospel reveals that life is always a mixed bag, *but a good mixed bag.* The kingdom "does not admit of [full] observation" here. Only in eternity are all shadows resolved. Here we live in faith and trust in the in-between.

REFLECT

In what ways does your goal orientation keep you from the journey to your goal itself?

Friday of the Third Week of Advent

Isaiah 56:1–3a, 6–8; John 5:33–36

—⁓—

> The works that the Father has given me to
> complete, the very works that I am doing,
> testify on my behalf that the Father has sent me.
>
> —JOHN 5:36

A BIAS TOWARD ACTION

Jesus says, "I am not asking you to just believe my words, look at my actions, or the 'works that I do.'" Actions speak for themselves, whereas words we can argue about on a theoretical level. The longer I have tried to follow Jesus, the more I can really say that I no longer *believe* in Jesus. I *know* Jesus. I know him because I have often taken his advice, taken his risks, and it always proves itself to be true! Afterward we do not believe, we *know*. Jesus is not telling us to believe unbelievable things, as if that would somehow please God. He is much more saying to us, "Try this" and you will see for yourself that it is true. But that initial trying is always a leap of faith into some kind of action or practice.

The Scriptures very clearly teach what we call today a "bias toward action." It is not just belief systems or dogmas and doctrines, as we have often made it. The Word of God is telling us very clearly that *if you do not do it, you, in fact, do not believe it and have not heard it.* The only way that we become convinced of our own sense of power, dignity and the power of God is by actually doing it—by crossing a line, a line that has a certain degree of non-sensicalness and unprovability to it—and that's why we call it faith. In the crossing of that line, and acting in a new way based on what we believe the kingdom values are, then and only then, can we hear in a new way and really believe what we say we believe in the first place.

In the years ahead I see Christianity moving from mere belief systems to an invitation to "practices" whereby we then realize things on a new level. (Jesuits call them "exercises," Methodists call them "methods," Gandhi called them "experiments with truth.")

Let me sum it up this way: *We do not think ourselves into a new way of living. We live ourselves into new ways of thinking.* Without action and lifestyle decisions, without concrete practices, words are dangerous and largely illusory.

REFLECT

What actions can you take to more fully realize the power of the Spirit?

December 17

Genesis 49:2, 8–10; Matthew 1:1–17

> "An account of the genealogy of Jesus"
> includes Tamar, Rahab, Ruth and "Uriah's
> wife" because they cannot bear to mention
> her name, Bathsheba.
>
> —MATTHEW 1:3, 5, 6, 7

THE AUTHORITY OF THOSE WHO HAVE SUFFERED

This artificially created family tree for Jesus is a brilliant theological statement much more than anything even remotely historically accurate. But the amazing thing is the deliberate inclusion of four foreign, non-Jewish women, of whom at least three were of easy virtue, or even public "sinners." Why would the Gospel risk saying that there were "horse thieves," as it were, among his ancestors? It clearly wanted to say that he came from the ordinary, the human, the broken, the sinful, suffering world, as all of us do. His birth accepted the full human condition, which becomes his first step toward the cross. It is that full and transformed humanity that gave Jesus authority in his actual lifetime. Remember, no one knew he was the Son of God; they trusted him for other reasons.

What gives any of us the practical authority to teach and preach and change lives? Is it ordination? Is it office? Is it family and ancestry? Is it vestment and title? Jesus did not have authority in his lifetime because of any external validation. He had it *because of the authenticity of his message and because of the transformative power of his journey through death to resurrection.* He had it because he was a genuine man of the Spirit. That is the basis of spiritual authority even today. More than any Scripture, sacrament or ordination, real authority comes from "drinking the cup that I must drink, and you also must drink" (Mark 10:38). Jesus seems to have made that rather clear, but for some reason we like to "sit on thrones on his left and right" (Mark 10:37).

Spiritually speaking, authority comes from passing through trial and darkness and coming out the other side even more free, happy, alive and contagious! *Transformed people transform people.* This is still true in our day. That is why Jesus came to preach the gospel "to the poor" because they are in a unique position to receive it in depth. For the suffering ones, salvation is not an abstract spiritual theory but a survival strategy. These are the people in "recovery" who have great power to influence you and change you, because "they speak with authority and not like the scribes" (Mark 1:22), who taught probably from seminary textbook knowledge. Where we ourselves have changed, suffered and been healed is where we are most in a position to be an effective change agent for others. After a while, that becomes pretty obvious.

REFLECT
What poverty can you find within yourself that may help you be more open to God?

December 18

Jeremiah 23:5–8; Matthew 1:18–25

> Joseph, son of David, do not be afraid to take Mary as your wife, for the child conceived in her is from the Holy Spirit.
> —MATTHEW 1:20

BREAKING OPEN THE WORD
We have a lot to learn from people like Quakers and Mennonites. They are well practiced in being a minority.

They don't need to have crowds around them to believe that it is the truth. They gather in little groups and share the Word of God. And that, thank God, is what is also happening again in the Catholic church. We call them the "base communities" of Latin America or the Bible study groups of America and Europe. Breaking open the Word of God cannot depend on people like me, theologians or people who have studied professionally. If that would be true, then 99 percent of humanity will never have access to God's Word.

These faith-sharing groups are directed not by a professional teacher or an expert, but rather what we call a facilitator or animator—one who holds the group together and knows what questions to ask to keep people searching and praying. The groups read a Gospel text, sometimes three times, and then they ask questions: What threatens them in the text? What makes them excited about that text? What is really challenging in that text? What do they think Jesus was really talking about? What was the world situation when Jesus told that particular story? Are there any comparable situations today to which this text might apply? Or perhaps in today's Gospel, "Do you really think Joseph understood what was happening? Was his trust in Mary, his dreams and the visions of angels really total certitude? Or was it actually faith?" Such questions are allowed and encouraged.

Whatever gave us the idea that one little select group of similarly educated people would best understand what God was to all people? The Word of God is being given back to the poor. The Word of God is being given back to the uneducated and the imprisoned. The Word of God is being given back to women. The Word of God is being given back to non-celibates (for us in the Catholic church). The Word of God is being given back to someone other than those who are the employees of the religious system. What we are finding is that the Word of God is being read with a vitality, a truth and often a freedom that is exciting, much more challenging and often making us wonder if we have ever understood it before. Just try it. This will not lessen the authority of the church or the Scriptures, but only increase it because we will have spiritual adults in our midst. Spiritual adults do not overreact or think dualistically, but they listen and learn and grow.

REFLECT

What simple messages from the Gospel are you missing?

Judges 13:2–7, 24–25a; Luke 1:5–25

—⁓—

> But they had no children, because
> Elizabeth was barren, and both were
> getting on in years.
>
> —LUKE 1:7

STAND-INS FOR SOCIAL ACCEPTABILITY

In today's readings we have two examples of barren or sterile women: the mother of Samson and Elizabeth, the mother of John the Baptist. The theme is so common among the wives of patriarchs that one begins to wonder if there was something wrong with the water in Israel. But maybe barrenness/fertility is a symbol of something else. Maybe all of the healing stories are not so much about medical cures as very real transformations. Jesus most often did not want people to talk about his physical cures. Does that surprise us? Do we know why? Because the mere medical cure was not the point, although most people stop there.

There are more healings of lepers than any other kind of story in the four Gospels. Jesus is always healing lepers.

Leprosy, in fact, in the New Testament is a broad term. It really doesn't mean what we would call Hansen's Disease today. "Lepers" were people who, for some reason, were told they were physically unacceptable. They were people who were considered taboo, contagious, disabled, dangerous or excluded for all kinds of reasons. The message seems to be: "You're not doing it right" or "You are not acceptable as a member of society." Every society does this, and we do too, but just in different ways and by different criteria.

When Jesus receives the lepers, he always touches them, and often he then leads them or sends them to a new place. Invariably he reintroduces them to the community and realigns their social status and acceptability. He pulls them back inside of social acceptability. *That is the healing!* The lepers are no longer disposable. The Gospel text also emphasizes Jesus' physical contact with the lepers, which of course makes *him* ritually unclean. Jesus' compassion is finally also an act of solidarity with the lepers' pain. He changes places with them, as it were. In several places the Gospel makes this explicit when it says that Jesus himself cannot now enter the city (see Mark 1:45).

Barren women and lepers are, of course, stand-ins for all of us as classic "before" pictures. Fertile women and realigned lepers are also stand-ins for all of us as the

triumphant "after" pictures. Authentic God encounters
make us all spiritually fertile and humanly connected.

REFLECT

Who do you know who has been rejected from your community and who you can reintroduce and thus heal?

December 20

Isaiah 7:10–14; Luke 1:26–38

—∭—

> She was much perplexed by [Gabriel's]
> words and pondered what sort of greeting
> this might be.
>
> —LUKE 1:29

A FEVERISH DESIRE FOR THE WILL OF GOD
Religious obedience means a willingness to let go of the
consequences on some level and to trust a Bigger Picture.
This is what we see Mary doing here in the great annunciation scene. In the obedience of faith we do something
because it is true at a deeper level, we feel called at a deeper

level perhaps, and not because it immediately works, makes sense or shows likelihood of "success." Often we have to let go of the immediate consequences to trust larger or longer-term consequences. Mother Teresa loved to say: "We were not created to be successful but to be obedient." Obedience is to be true to our deepest voices, which is the only way God can speak to us. But that means we have to *have* some deeper voices! We have to be practiced in prayerfully listening to our unconscious, to others and even "entertaining angels who usually come unaware" (Hebrews 13:2). How else could Mary have been ready for Gabriel?

Sooner or later we all have to say, "I have to do what I have to do," as did Franz Jägerstätter, the Austrian peasant who almost single-handedly opposed Hitler. Have you ever been caught that way by the Word of God? "I just know I have to do it. My family doesn't understand, my friends criticize me, but I know it is the Word planted in my heart for me at this time." One must feel very lonely and filled with doubt at such times. Yet, after all is said and done, *the will of God, more than anything else, is the feverish desire to do the will of God.* People who are centered in God instead of themselves always hear larger voices. Such people will know what they must do without being able to prove it. They have the passion to carry through on what must be done. Blessed Franz

Jägerstätter was not supported by his church, church teaching, his bishop, his parish priest or even his wife (she told me so personally, with tears in her eyes!).

Mary's "yes" was said in the darkness of faith. She was not certain, nor assured by any Scripture quote, doctrine or pope. She just heard what she heard, and did what God asked her to do, accepting the consequences. She had enough inner authority to not need a lot of outer authority.

REFLECT

In what way do you have a feverish desire to do the will of God?

December 21

Song of Songs 2:18–14 or Zephaniah 3:14–18a; Luke 1:39–45

> And blessed is she who believed that there
> would be a fulfillment of what was spoken
> to her by the Lord.
>
> —LUKE 1:45

TRUE RELIGION

When it comes to the gift of contemplation, every major religion in the world has come to very similar conclusions. Every religion—Hinduism, Judaism, Buddhism, the eastern religions—all agree, but each in its own way, that finally we're called to a transformed consciousness, a new mind or being "born again" a second time in some way. Each religion has different words for it, and probably different experiences, but somehow they all point to union with God. Religion is about union. Somehow to live in conscious union with God is what it means to be "saved."

The word *religio* means "to retie"—to rebind reality together, to reconnect things so that we know as Jesus did that "I and the Father are one" (John 10:30). To live in that place is to experience and enjoy the Great Connection, to live in a place where all things are one, "with me in them and you in me" (John 17:23). When world religions become that mature, we will have a new history, no longer based on competition, rivalry, cultures or warfare, but on people who are actually transformed (Galatians 6:15-16). These people will change the world, as Mary did, almost precisely because they know it is not they who are doing the changing. They will know they do not need to change other people, just themselves. God takes it from there.

How can you bring the gift of contemplation into your prayer life?

December 22

1 Samuel 1:24–28; Luke 1:46–56

—⁓—

...[God] has scattered the proud in the
thoughts of their hearts.
He has brought down the powerful from
their thrones,
and lifted up the lowly;
he has filled the hungry with good things,
and sent the rich away empty.

—LUKE 1:51-53

POWER, PRESTIGE AND POSSESSIONS

In Jesus' consistent teaching and in Mary's great Magnificat, both say that there are three major obstacles to the coming of the reign of God. I call them the three P's: power, prestige and possessions. Mary refers to them as "the proud," "the mighty on thrones" and "the rich." These, she says, God is "routing," "pulling down" and "sending away empty." (This great prayer of Mary was considered so subversive by the Argentine government that they banned it from public recitation at protest marches!) We can easily take nine-tenths of Jesus' teachings and very clearly align it under one of those three categories: Our attachments to power, prestige and possessions are obstacles to God's coming. Why could we not see that?

For some reason, we tend to localize evil in our bodies more than in our mind, heart and spirit. We are terribly ashamed of our embodiment, and our shame is invariably located in addictive things like drinking, drugs, sex, overeating and body image. Maybe that is why God had to become *a body* in Jesus! God needed to tell us it was good to be a human body. That is central and pivotal to the Christmas message.

I'm surely for a proper sexual morality, but Jesus never once says this is the core issue. They tend to be sins of weakness or addiction, more than malice or power. In fact, Jesus says that the "prostitutes are getting into the kingdom of God" before some of us who have made easy bedfellows with power, prestige and possessions (Matthew 21:31). These are the attitudes that numb the heart, allow us to make very egocentric judgments and dull our general spiritual perception.

For some reason, much of Christian history has chosen not to see this, and we have localized evil in other places than Jesus did. It is the sins of our mind and heart (see Matthew 5:20-48) that make the Big Picture almost impossible to see. This teaching is hidden in plain sight, but once we see it in text after text, we cannot any longer unsee it. Mary seems to have seen long, deep and lovely.

REFLECT

How are power, prestige and possessions preventing you from entering the kingdom?

December 23

Malachi 3:1–4, 23–24; Luke 1:57–66

—⟁—

> For he is like a refiner's fire and like fullers'
> soap;...he will purify the descendants of
> Levi.... Lo, I will send you the prophet
> Elijah before the great and terrible day of
> the Lord comes. He will turn the hearts of

parents to their children and the hearts
of children to their parents....

—MALACHI 3:2-3, 23-24

CONFRONTATION, CONVERSION, CONSOLATION

These words from the prophet Malachi are the last words in
our Old Testament, and they provide a perfect segue to the
New Testament. They describe the one who will be the fit-
ting precursor for any coming Messiah. Christians have, of
course, usually applied this passage to John the Baptist, as
Jesus himself and the Gospel writers already had done. But
the text has even more significance: In a very few verses it
succeeds in charting the appropriate sequencing of the
Word of God. When the Scriptures are used maturely, and
they become a precursor to meeting the Christ, they pro-
ceed in this order:

1. They *confront* us with a bigger picture than we are
   used to, "God's kingdom" that has the potential to
   "deconstruct" our false world views.
2. They then have the power to *convert* us to an alternative worldview by proclamation, grace and the sheer
   attraction of the good, the true and the beautiful (not by
   shame, guilt or fear which are low-level motivations).

"Attraction not promotion," said Bill Wilson, co-founder of Alcoholics Anonymous.

3. They then *console* us and bring deep healing as they "reconstruct" us in a new place with a new mind and heart.

Malachi does this. He describes the work of the God Messenger as both "great and terrible," both wonderful and threatening at the same time. It is not that the Word of God is threatening us with fire and brimstone, but rather it is saying that *goodness is its own reward and evil is its own punishment.* If we do the truth and live connected in the world as it really is, we will be blessed and grace can flow, and the consolation will follow from the confrontation with the Big Picture. If we create a false world of separateness and egocentricity, it will not work and we will suffer the consequences even now. In Catholic theology we call this our tradition of "natural law." In short, we are not punished *for* our sins, but *by* our sins!

We are always the "stable" into which the Christ is born anew. All we can really do is keep our stable honest and humble, and the Christ will surely be born.

Reflect

Find a Gospel passage that you look to for consolation and let it challenge you.

Fourth Sunday of Advent

Year A: Isaiah 7:10–14; Romans 1:1–7; Matthew 1:18–24

Year B: 2 Samuel 7:1–5, 8b–12, 14a, 16; Romans 16:25–27;
          Luke 1:26–38

Year C: Micah 5:1–4a; Hebrews 10:5–10; Luke 1:39–45

—⟨⟨⟨—

> Therefore the Lord himself will give you a
> sign. Look, the young woman is with child
> and shall bear a son, and shall name him
> Immanuel.
>
> —ISAIAH 7:14

THE BLIND FAITH OF MARY AND JOSEPH

Kingdom people are history makers. They break through the
small kingdoms of this world to an alternative and much
larger world, God's full creation. People who are still living in
the false self are history stoppers. They use God and religion
to protect their own status and the status quo of the world
that sustains them. They are often fearful people, the nice

proper folks of every age who think like everybody else thinks and who have no power to break through, or as Jesus' opening words put it, "to change" (Mark 1:15, Matthew 4:17).

How can we really think that Mary, if she thought like any good Jewish girl was trained to think, could possibly be ready for this message? She had to let God lead her outside of her box of expectations, her comfort zone, her dutiful religion of follow-the-leader. She was very young and largely uneducated. Perhaps theology itself is not the necessary path but simply integrity and courage. Nothing said at the synagogue would have prepared Mary or Joseph for this situation. They both had to rely on their angels! What proper bishop would trust such a situation? I wouldn't myself. All we know of Joseph is that he was "a just man" (Matthew 1:19), also young and probably uneducated. This is all an affront to our criteria and way of evaluating authenticity.

So why do we love and admire people like Mary and Joseph, and then not imitate their faith journeys, their courage, their non-reassurance by the religious system? These were two laypeople who totally trusted their inner experience of God and who followed it to Bethlehem and beyond. There is no mention in the Gospels of the two checking out their inner experiences with the high priests, the synagogue or even their Jewish Scriptures. Mary and

Joseph walked in courage and blind faith that their experience was true, with no one to reassure them they were right. Their only safety net was God's love and mercy, a safety net they must have tried out many times, or else they would never have been able to fall into it so gracefully.

REFLECT

In what ways do you trust your own inner authority? Do you fear you are being rebellious if you do so? Were Mary and Joseph rebellious?

December 24, Christmas Eve

Morning: 2 Samuel 7:1–5, 8b–12, 14a, 16; Luke 1:67–79

Vigil: Isaiah 62:1–5; Acts 13:16–17, 22–25; Matthew 1:1–25 or 1:18–25

—⟋𝔪⟍—

Go and tell my servant David..."Are you the
one to build me a house to live in?"... I took
you from the pasture,...I have been with
you wherever you went, and have cut off
all your enemies from before you; and I will

make for you a great name,... I will appoint
a place for my people Israel,...the LORD
declares to you that the LORD will make you
a house.... Your house and your kingdom
shall be made sure for ever before me; your
throne shall be established for ever.

—2 Samuel 7:5, 8, 9, 10, 11, 16

ALL IS IN READINESS

Probably not many people read meditations on Christmas
Eve morning, so I congratulate you for taking time to do so
when I know there must be so many exciting and anticipa-
tory things to do today. All is in readiness. There is probably no day of the year which has so much expectation as
December 24. It is really more Christmas than Christmas
Day itself because it holds the full energy of Advent. Time
has come to its fullness (Luke 2:6). Hardly anybody comes
to church this morning. It is all about tonight for some
wonderful reason.

This is unfortunate, however, because the first reading
of today's morning Mass is especially poignant, and actually one of my favorites, but hardly anyone hears it today.
The reading is a wonderful dialogue between the prophet
Nathan and King David, part of which we read above. This

changing of sides is the great turnaround, which henceforth becomes the central Biblical theme of grace, election and Divine initiative. We set out, like David, thinking we have to do something to prove ourselves to God, "build God a house" is the metaphor. And as always, God turns it around and says, "No, David, let me build *you* a house!" (If you wish, read all of 2 Samuel 7, as it is quite lovely.)

It is time to let that story soak into our unconscious. It will prepare us fully for the day ahead, much more than anything I could say.

REFLECT

Are you still trying to build God a house, or can you first let God build one for you?

December 25, Christmas Day

Midnight: Isaiah 9:1–6; Titus 2:11–14; Luke 2:1–14

Dawn: Isaiah 62:11–12; Titus 3:4–7; Luke 2:15–20

Day: Isaiah 52:7–10; Hebrews 1:1–6; John 1:1–18
           or 1:1–5, 9–14

———

And the Word became flesh and lived
among us, and we have seen his glory, the
glory as of a father's only son, full of grace
and truth.

—JOHN 1:14

SOMEONE TO SURRENDER TO

On this Christmas Day, let me begin with a quote from
twentieth-century writer G.K. Chesterton: "When a person
has found something which he prefers to life itself, he (sic) for
the first time has begun to live." Jesus in his proclamation of
the kingdom told us what we could prefer to life itself—and it

would work! The Bible ends by telling us we are called to be a people who could say, "Come, Lord Jesus" (Revelation 22:20), who could welcome something more than business as usual and live in God's Big Picture. We all have to ask for the grace to prefer something to our small life itself because we have been offered the shared Life, the One Life, the Eternal Life, God's Life that became visible in this world in Jesus. We do not get there by being correct. We get there by allowing the connection. It is like a "free wireless" connection!

The kingdom is finally to be identified as the Lord Jesus himself. When we say "Come, Lord Jesus" on this Christmas Day, we are preferring his Lordship to any other loyalty system or any other final frame of reference. If Jesus is Lord, than Caesar is not! If Jesus is Lord, then the economy and stock market are not! If Jesus is Lord, then my house and possessions, family and job are not! If Jesus is Lord, than I am not! That multileveled implication was obvious to first-century members of the Roman Empire because the phrase "Caesar is Lord" was the empire's loyalty test and political bumper sticker. They, and others, knew they had changed "parties" when they welcomed Jesus as Lord instead of the Roman emperor as their savior.

What we are all searching for is Someone to surrender to, something we can prefer to life itself. Well here is the wonderful surprise: God is the only one we can surrender to without losing ourselves. The irony is that we find ourselves, and now in a whole new field of meaning. This happens on a lesser level in every great love in our lifetime, but it is always a leap of faith ahead of time. We are never sure it will be true beforehand. It is surely counter-intuitive, but it is the promise that came into the world on this Christmas Day, "full of grace and of truth." Jesus is the gift totally given, free for the taking, once and for all, to everybody and all of creation. This Cosmic Risen Christ really is *free wireless*, and all we have to do is connect.

Henceforth humanity has the right to know that it is *good to be human, good to live on this earth, good to have a body*, because God in Jesus chose and said "yes" to our humanity. Or as we Franciscans love to say, "Incarnation is already Redemption." The problem is solved. Now go and utterly enjoy all remaining days. Not only is it "Always Advent," but every day can now be Christmas because the one we thought we were just waiting for has come *once and for all.*

REFLECT

Today just "taste and see the goodness of the Lord" (Psalm 34:8)!

*Preparing for Christmas
With Richard Rohr:
Daily Reflections for Advent*

is also available in a
SPANISH-LANGUAGE EDITION:

*Preparándose para Navidad
Con P. Richard Rohr, O.F.M.:
Reflexiones Diarias para Adviento*

Item number B16903 $1.95 each
(quantity discounts available)

To order, call: 1-513-241-5615
Toll-free: 1-800-488-0488
Order online at: www.SAMPBooks.org.